Life + Soul
LIBRARY

Why do I have to eat my greens?

Big issues for little people about health and well-being

Written by **Dr. Emma Waddington** + **Dr. Christopher McCurry**

Illustrated by **Louis Thomas**

Frances Lincoln
Children's Books

Contents

How to use this book

This book has been conceived for you to share with a child. Each spread is themed by topic and should be used as a discussion point to help you to talk through common issues in childhood.

STEP 1   Turn to the spread featuring the issue you wish to discuss with a child.

STEP 2   Before sitting down with the child, read the advice from the authors explaining some common causes of behavioral patterns, and some tips on how to tackle them.

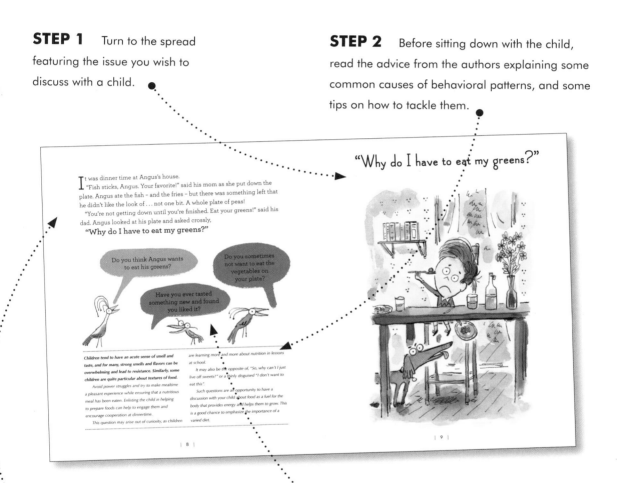

STEP 3   Direct the child's attention to the illustration and read the story that accompanies the scenario in front of them. This is a safe and nonconfrontational way to approach a topic.

STEP 4   Explore the issue further with the conversational prompts that encourage the child to empathize with the scenario. This should ease you in to having a conversation with them about their own behavior.

"Finish your dinner!" said Dad, but Angus pushed away his plate and asked crossly, "Why do I have to eat my greens?"

How will this book help you talk to a child?

Children love to ask questions. A four-year-old girl can reportedly ask up to 390 questions a day, which adds up to over 100,000 questions a year! Curiosity is an essential ingredient for a child's developing brain, and our response plays a key part in that development.

Most questions from children are pretty mundane, but now and again they will ask something that leaves us dumbfounded, surprised, or, at times, upset, meaning that we cannot answer without further thought and time. In this book, we will explain some commonly asked questions from children, offer advice on how to respond (and explain why your answers matter!) and talk about how to manage the emotions that may come with these discussions. If you need further support in certain areas, turn to the back of this book where you will find resources to help you.

Why are children curious about their world?

Children are natural explorers. Exploring is a reflex when they are very young; they reach out and observe objects in their surroundings. As they grow and are able to move and manipulate their environment, exploring becomes more exciting and rewarding to them; they will poke, pick, chew, hit, throw, lick, and grab just about anything that is around them!

Children independently seek to understand and discover their environment, which helps them develop theories and understandings of their world. As they explore and their brains grow, their natural curiosity leads them to ask questions.

These early years are the most important for a child's

> Children independently seek to understand and discover their environment

brain, setting the ground for future growth. The brain is at its most receptive, and it is learning faster and changing in response to new experiences more efficiently.

How is a child's behavior connected to their developing brain?

As children explore and learn, they are building their brain – in particular, the front of their brains. This is the part that helps us make sense of our world.

In adults, the front part of the brain is huge, and this allows us to override the reactive back of the brain in order to slow down, reason, evaluate, and make sense of situations and experiences.

However, up to the age of four, it is the back of a child's brain that dominates. This back part of the brain – also known as our reptilian brain – is responsible for letting us know when something bad is happening and informing us that we need to run away. This is a reactive part of the brain that was once essential for survival, and is, by nature, very inflexible, which is why it can be so hard to calm a tantrum in full blast.

Unfortunately the front and back of the brain are poorly connected – especially in the very young. So when the amygdala, the specific part of the reptilian brain responsible for emotions such as fear and anger, fires up, it is very hard to tame.

As carers, we want our children to develop the front of the brain, as this will help them manage their behavior. This means that we can reason with them when they are in the midst of a fierce tantrum; we can ask them to wait, and they will, before jumping out onto the road, and so on.

So as children ask questions and hear your answers, these experiences are also shaping their brains – in particular their frontal lobes. As they build these networks, our children will be better able to manage social situations, build stronger bonds, and act in ways that bring them joy and happiness.

> We want our children to develop the front of their brain, as this will help them manage their behavior

Why are the answers to a child's questions important?

You are a child's first source of "truth" in the world, and are responsible for shaping their beliefs, concerns, views, values, and principles concerning how to behave . . . And the values you instill in a child now will probably continue to influence them for the rest of their life. By "values" we mean what a child will find important, meaningful, and fulfilling in life: the direction they will want to take. We can also see it as their point of reference or a compass, that will help them navigate through some of life's choppy waters.

Often, when we work with parents and families, we ask them to spend time thinking about what they want for their children. Most parents will initially answer, "happiness." Yet when we ask them to explore further what will lead their children to feel happy, parents talk about "being independent," "being a good friend," "being healthy," or "being a good student." With these values in tow, as parents we are then better able to keep focused on what really matters when we are in the midst of the torrent of questions and heightened emotions – both theirs and ours. We will invite you to think about your values as you answer the questions throughout the book.

How can you encourage a child to reason and cooperate through conversation?

This is one of the problems parents regularly face. At times, a child's incessant questions might seem like a stalling tactic, or as if they are being pedantic. Questions like, "Why do I have to go to bed?" are often charged with emotion, and, because feelings originate in the back of the brain, reasoning, at first, can be very difficult.

Instead, as we'll see, our initial intervention will be to name the emotion, acknowledge it, and connect with it in that moment. Statements such as, "I understand that this is really upsetting you" or, "You seem to be getting frustrated" validate a child's emotion, and help them understand the emotion they are experiencing. This, in turn, will help the back of the brain to calm down and improve the chance of connecting

> **You are a child's first source of "truth" in the world**

with their developing frontal lobe.

Once a child feels you are listening, you can start to engage the frontal lobe and attempt to reason with them. Try to explain the reasons you can't or won't negotiate, or perhaps even find a way to compromise.

Why should you talk to a child about self-care?

We understand that keeping a child healthy matters to you – and that sometimes this can be a challenge! Children, when they are young, don't really understand what is healthy and good for them. These long-term values seem very remote to young children, who have immature frontal lobes and can't think further ahead.

With this book, we aim to help you teach a child that self-care and health are important in keeping them strong and fit, by focusing on values that matter to them in the short term (like being able to see like Superman, or dance like a ballerina). We have an opportunity in these early years to set some good to routines and habits that a child will maintain in their adult years.

> # Long-term values about health and self-care seem very remote to young children

By finding ways to encourage a child's curiosity as they question the need for self-care, we will be activating their brains in different ways . . .

By giving them reasons that are consistent with what matters to them in that moment, we will be helping them find meaning in their actions.

By helping them feel understood and heard, we will be helping you to manage some of the emotions that arise.

By being consistent in your expectations and setting good routines, you will be communicating the importance in these actions.

Together we will work on making you feel more confident in navigating the torrent of questions that we are faced with daily, with commitment and care.

We look forward to working in this new way together!

It was dinner time at Angus's house.

"Fish sticks, Angus. Your favorite!" said his mom as she put down the plate. Angus ate the fish – and the fries – but there was something left that he didn't like the look of . . . not one bit. A whole plate of peas!

"You're not getting down until you're finished. Eat your greens!" said his dad. Angus looked at his plate and asked crossly,

"Why do I have to eat my greens?"

Do you think Angus wants to eat his greens?

Do you sometimes not want to eat the vegetables on your plate?

Have you ever tasted something new and found you liked it?

Children tend to have an acute sense of smell and taste, and for many, strong smells and flavors can be overwhelming and lead to resistance. Similarly, some children are quite particular about textures of food.

Avoid power struggles and try to make mealtime a pleasant experience while ensuring that a nutritious meal has been eaten. Enlisting the child in helping to prepare foods can help to engage them and encourage cooperation at dinnertime.

This question may arise out of curiosity, as children are learning more and more about nutrition in lessons at school.

It may also be the opposite of, "So, why can't I just live off sweets?" or a thinly disguised "I don't want to eat this".

Such questions are an opportunity to have a discussion with your child about food as a fuel for the body that provides energy and helps them to grow. This is a good chance to emphasize the importance of a varied diet.

"Why do I have to eat my greens?"

It was bedtime at Ibrahim's house, but he wasn't sleepy.
"Dad?" he called. "Daaad!"

"What is it, Ibrahim?" asked his dad, putting his head around the door. "I've read you a story, I've brought you some water, and I've taken you to the toilet. I've come upstairs three times already. Now it's bedtime and you need to go to sleep." But Ibrahim crossed his arms and asked,

"Why do have to go to bed at night?"

Do you think Ibrahim looks sleepy?

Do you sometimes feel like you don't want to go to sleep?

What would you do if you stayed up all night long?

One reason for questions such as this is simple curiosity: what is sleep?

Describe sleep to the child as a necessary part of the day's (night's) activities that allows our brain to rest, and our body to relax and restore itself to be ready for another day.

Another reason for these questions is a bit of anxiety about the separation from the parent, a fear of the dark, or other ideas brought on by the night. If you suspect anxiety you may ask the child to describe their *emotions and ideas. Often some simple reassurances of the child's safety and your continued availability ("I'll check on you in ten minutes") can suffice. At times, however, this can become an endless series of questions, pleas, and negotiations. Staying with the child in a dimly lit room, without conversation, can allow the child to develop the habit of going to sleep in their own bed in a reasonable amount of time.*

"Why do I have to go to bed at night?"

It was nighttime at Angus's house. He had woken up to go to the bathroom, but instead of going back to his own bed, he tiptoed to his mom and dad's room.

"Mom? Dad? Are you awake?" he asked in a whisper, tugging at his mom's sleeve. His mom woke with a start.

"Angus!" she said in surprise. "What are you doing up? You should be in bed, fast asleep." But Angus didn't want to go back to his own bed, and asked,

"Why can't I sleep with you?"

What do you think Angus is thinking right now?

What do you think about when you wake up at night?

What would help you to go back to sleep in your own bed?

Co-sleeping is a growing phenomenon: currently 13 percent of households in the U.S. subscribe to this idea.

This is a personal choice each family must make for themselves. Because good sleep is so important, one should first and foremost consider what gives everyone the best night's sleep, as some children (and grown-ups) do better sleeping on their own.

This question of sleeping with a parent may arise because an older child is observing an infant sibling *sleeping with parents as a way of making nighttime feedings easier. Or, the child may wish to forestall being alone for the night.*

Before answering the question, gently explore what may lie behind it in terms of ideas or emotions: jealousy, curiosity, anxiety? Validate these ideas and feelings and then remind the child of your rules and expectations about sleep. Again, spending a little time in the room with the child while they allow themselves to fall asleep can help establish this habit.

"Why can't I sleep with you?"

It was the middle of the night at Yuki's house. Yuki had been fast asleep, having a dream about riding a pony. In her dream, she had needed to pee, and had gone to the toilet, and then something had woken her up . . . A hot, wet feeling. She called her mom into her bedroom.

"Yuki, have you wet the bed?" her mom asked. "Remember, when you need to pee in the night, you have to get up and use the toilet." Yuki replied,

"Why can't I wet the bed?"

> Do you think Yuki's mother was expecting to see a wet bed?

> Do you like having a clean, dry bed to sleep in?

> What do we expect you to do at night if you need to go?

How this question is managed will depend on the reason it's being asked.

Is the child simply curious about this social convention of not wetting the bed? If so, one can simply explain that it is too messy and smelly to be using the bed as a convenient nighttime toilet.

Is the child fearful of leaving his bed to venture into the bathroom in the middle of the night? Some well-placed night-lights could help.

Finally, if the child is experiencing enuresis,

or nighttime bed wetting, then a compassionate conversation about remedying the situation, with the help of one's pediatrician, would be a place to start. Emphasize that this is not the child's fault and there are steps you and the child can take to address the problem.

If the child feels supported and cared for it will go a long way to reduce embarrassment and increase cooperation with any program you implement.

"Why can't I wet the bed?"

Angus was in the car, on the way to Grandma's house. He didn't like car journeys. They were so boring!

"What are you doing, Angus?" asked Mom, turning around, looking cross.

"Sit still!" said Dad. But Angus couldn't see why he had to sit there with the silly seat belt on, and shouted,

"Why do I have to wear a seat belt?"

How do you think Angus feels about wearing his seat belt?

Do you sometimes feel that way?

Tell me about some other ways we stay safe.

Many children like to move and will resist being confined, perhaps not right away but after a period of time in the car or on an airplane.

Some children resist wearing a helmet while riding a bike for a variety of reasons, ranging from comfort to wanting to look "cool" – or at least, not "uncool."

The potential consequences for not wearing one's seat belt or helmet, like so many other issues of safety, are likely beyond the imagination of a young child. There is no need to fill their minds with visions of horrible accidents. Simply state that these steps are part of – a condition of – being able to do these activities. Children have to follow these rules just as grown-ups follow rules when they drive a car, or do any activity where bodies must be protected while moving from one place to another very fast. Just as we are careful about what we put into our bodies and our minds, we protect our bodies from possible accidents as best we can.

"Why do I have to wear a seat belt?"

It was the end of the day at Olivia's house and Olivia was still out, playing in the garden with her dog, Raffles. She was very muddy and having lots of fun – and she didn't want to finish her game.

"Upstairs, Olivia!" called Olivia's mommy. "It's bathtime!" But Olivia didn't want to have a bath. She stomped up the stairs into the bathroom and asked her mom,

"What happens if I don't bathe at night?"

Do you think Olivia enjoys her bath time?

What helps make bath time fun?

If it's not so fun, how can we make it go quickly and safely?

This question, like so many we encounter, may stem from either curiosity or an attempt at exercising some control over the evening routine.

Assume it's curiosity and respond with something like, "That's a good question. Let me think about it for a moment while you get your clothes off/into the tub."

Give a matter-of-fact, age-appropriate answer such as, "If we didn't bathe (or brush our teeth or wash our hair) we would just collect dirt on ourselves and we wouldn't feel fresh and we might begin to smell a bit." Then redirect the child to the next step in the routine.

The idea of germs can be a mysterious and scary topic for some children and may potentially set off anxieties. Casually explain that germs are all around us, but they are no match for a clean body. Giving a child some control over the process, such as setting the pace of events (so long as it's reasonable) can help them feel less fearful and more empowered, as well as understood.

"What happens if I don't bathe at night?"

Ibrahim was getting ready for bed and was in the bathroom. Every evening (and every morning, too!) his mom would call up the stairs to remind him to brush his teeth. It seemed a bit boring to do the same thing, day after day, and sometimes he wondered to himself,

"Why must I brush my teeth?"

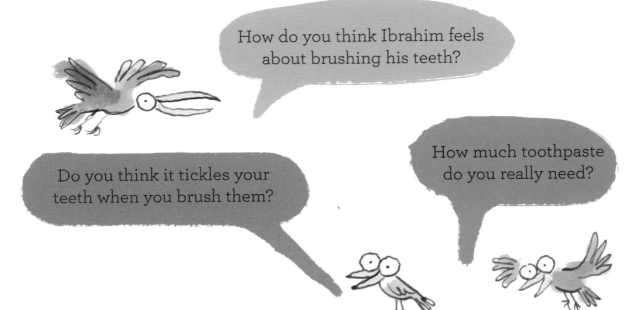

How do you think Ibrahim feels about brushing his teeth?

Do you think it tickles your teeth when you brush them?

How much toothpaste do you really need?

Here, too, questions may be born out of curiosity or may be a subtle (or not so subtle) attempt to evade a tiresome chore.

Parents can explain that, like keeping our skin and hair clean and fresh, we must maintain the bits on the inside.

The teeth reside in an in-between space: others see them when we talk and laugh and smile but our teeth are often hidden away behind our lips. They must be ready for an appearance at any time!

It's probably best not to provide a young child with vivid descriptions of oral bacteria eating away at their teeth in the dark of night. This might lead to unnecessary anxieties.

Providing a consistent bedtime routine that includes brushing teeth together and other self-care tasks in anticipation of a story and a cuddle can help move children through these procedures with a minimum of fussing.

"Why must I brush my teeth?"

It was Halloween, and Angus was out trick-or-treating with his dad. He knocked on every door on the street, and each neighbor dropped some sweets into his bucket. On their way home, with his bucket full to the brim with treats, his dad turned to him and said, "You mustn't eat those all at once, Angus. You can't eat sweets all the time!" But Angus couldn't see why that should be, and asked,

"Why can't I eat sweets all the time?"

What answer do you imagine his parents will give him?

Can you imagine if all we ever ate were sweets, for every meal?

How do you think Angus would feel if he ate all of those sweets?

Children live in a "here-and-now" world; they want what they want, here and now.

Delaying gratification and working toward distant goals are signs of maturity that many adults struggle with. Teaching children these character traits is the valued goal of many parents and caregivers.

Questions such as this call for acknowledging the positive side of the desire ("Yes, that would be delicious!") while placing your answer within a larger context of promoting healthy choices: "And, we must

be thoughtful about what we put in our bodies, which means having lots of good, healthy things to eat and not a lot of things that may taste good but don't help our bodies grow in a healthy way."

Acknowledge the disappointment and then change the topic. Finally, caregivers who model good eating themselves help children to learn these values and habits. Think out loud about your choices, acknowledging dilemmas: "I'd love to have a second piece of that yummy cake, but I think not."

"Why can't I eat sweets all the time?"

It was after school at Abby's house, and she was watching cartoons. She was in the middle of her favorite program when her mom called her into the kitchen.

"Abby! Time to turn the TV off. Come and tell me what you did at school." But Abby didn't want to – she wanted to keep watching her program. She shouted back,

"Why do you always tell me to turn the television off?"

Do you think Abby should watch any more TV for the night?

Why is it so hard to stop watching TV?

What about her dog?

Television, along with video and computer games, seems to place a hypnotic spell on a child that can be very hard to break.

Establishing clear rules, schedules, and expectations for "screen time" can help when it's time to transition to another activity.

This will help establish good habits and create expectations for time limits. Young children may not have the time concepts yet to appreciate that ten or twenty minutes has just flown by. Setting timers can

help. A few minutes' warning is only fair but then the caregiver gets the child's attention (eye contact) and makes a matter-of-fact declaration that the time is up, the device must go off, and we're on to the next thing. Empathize with the child's disappointment or frustration: "I know, you were really enjoying that game."

Giving the child a job to do – "Here, I need you to please carry these towels into the bathroom" – can help with the transition.

"Why do you always tell me to turn the television off?"

Yuki and her dog, Inu, were outside playing in the garden. The sky clouded over, and before long, it was raining hard. But Yuki didn't mind – she loved playing in the mud! Just then the backdoor opened and her mom called out, "Yuki, come back inside and put your raincoat on!" But Yuki didn't want to stop playing, and called back,

"Why do I have to wear a coat when it's raining?"

Do you think Yuki is happy to be getting all wet?

Would you like to be out in a storm?

How do you know that it might rain?

Many children love to play in the rain, to splash in puddles, to feel free and a bit reckless in a safe way.

As with the later question about sunscreen, this is an opportunity for teaching a child about protecting ourselves from the elements.

We wear raincoats, hats, and boots so that we can enjoy this weather in relative comfort. Additionally, these situations are an opportunity to help a child anticipate events, to do some planning and problem solving: "Does it look like it might rain?"; "How would we feel if we were to be all soaked through halfway to the market?"; "Should we take an umbrella, just in case?"

In these ways we can help children think about consequences and empower them to solve problems, all the while showing them we are attentive to their ideas and concerns, and always there to provide guidance and security.

"Why do I have to wear a coat when it's raining?"

It was summer vacation and Angus's family had gone to the beach. This was one of Angus's favorite things to do! He loved making sandcastles and playing in the waves. The only problem was that his mom kept calling him over to rub sunscreen on him, because of the hot sun. Angus didn't want to stop playing and asked her,

"Why do I have to wear sunscreen when it's sunny?"

What happened to Angus? Why is he so pink?

What does it feel like to have sunscreen rubbed on your skin?

Do you think the sun is shining even when the sky is cloudy?

Children are impatient creatures. They want what they want NOW. So, getting ready to go outside and play can be a very frustrating experience, for both parent and child.

Be firm about the sunscreen rule and offer some validation of the child's impatience along with a simple "here-and-now" reason for the sunscreen ritual. For example, "I see that you're very eager to get outside and putting on sunscreen is annoying. But it's important to protect our skin so that we can enjoy the sun now and not feel uncomfortable later."

Or use the "when-then" approach: "When we get the sunscreen on, then we can go outside." Call it "sun paint" and use a soft, clean paint brush to apply the lotion. Make sunscreen a habit when spending time outside.

Be a good role model by routinely using sunscreen yourself. This builds credibility for you as an authority on important self-care issues.

"Why do I have to wear sunscreen when it's sunny?"

Abby's dad had a friend over for dinner. Abby had some water with her food, but her dad and his friend were drinking something else. She asked her dad what it was, and if she could try some too.

"This is wine, Abby, but you can't have any. Wine is for grown-ups," her dad answered. Abby couldn't understand why that should be and asked,

"Why can't I have some of your wine?"

Why do you think Abby wants to drink some of her Daddy's wine?

What do you think her parents will say?

Do you ever think about what you want to do when you get to be a grown-up?

Sooner or later children will ask about all sorts of adult behaviors; the more adultlike and mysterious the behavior, the more they provoke a child's curiosity.

Some families do not partake in alcohol and so this question may never come up. In other families, children may be allowed a sip of wine on special occasions. All depends on the values and traditions within the family.

Such questions may be cause for parents to do a

bit of reflecting on their values and ideals, their own habits, and the example they wish to set for a child. For the young child, simple answers are best: this is another choice about what we put into our bodies, grown-ups sometimes eat and drink things that don't help young brains and bodies grow in healthy ways.

For an older child, as with the sweets, one must acknowledge the pleasant aspects of the experience while emphasizing self-discipline and self-care as important goals.

"Why can't I have some of your wine?"

Further reading and resources

NUTRITION
Books to read with children
Child, L. *I Will Never Not Ever Eat a Tomato* (Somerville, MA: Candlewick Press, 2001)

Llewellyn, C. *Why Should I Eat Well?* (Hauppauge, NY: Barron's Educational Books, 2005)

Websites
choosemyplate.gov. U.S. Department of Agriculture: nutritional information and healthy eating tips

healthychildren.org. American Academy of Pediatrics: information about child development and health

SELF-CARE
Books to read with children
Schaefer, V. *The Care and Keeping of You: The Body Book for Younger Girls* (Middleton, WI: American Girl Publishing, 2012)

Wrobel, M. *Taking Care of Myself: A Hygiene, Puberty and Personal Curriculum for Young People with Autism*. (Arlington, TX: Future Horizons, 2003)

Websites
csefel.vanderbilt.edu/documents/teaching_routines.pdf Vanderbilt University Center on the Social and Emotional Foundations for Early Learning

SLEEP
Books to read with children
Boynton, S. *The Going to Bed Book* (New York: Little Simon Publishing, 1982)

Child, L. *I Am Not Sleepy and I Will Not Go to Bed* (Somerville, MA: Candlewick Press, 2005)

Huebner, D. *What to Do When You Dread Your Bed: A Kid's Guide to Overcoming Problems With Sleep (What to Do Guides for Kids)* (Washington, D.C.: Magination Press, 2008)

Owens, J. A., & Mindell, J. A. *Take Charge of Your Child's Sleep: The All-in-One Resource for Solving Sleep Problems in Kids and Teens* (New York: Marlowe & Company, 2005)

Websites
sleepforkids.org. Sponsored by the National Sleep Foundation.

sleepfoundation.org/sleep-disorders-problems. Information about bedwetting, the relationship between ADHD and sleep, and other topics.

parenting.com. Information and advice on a wide variety of topics, including talking to children about sleep and tips for helping children sleep on their own.

Why do I have to eat my greens? copyright © Frances Lincoln Limited 2016
Text copyright © Dr. Emma Waddington and Dr. Christopher McCurry 2016
Illustrations copyright © Louis Thomas 2016

First published in the USA in 2016 by Frances Lincoln Children's Books,
an imprint of Quarto Inc., 276 Fifth Avenue, Suite 206, New York, NY 10001
QuartoKnows.com • Visit our blogs at QuartoKnows.com

Edited by Jenny Broom • Designed by Andrew Watson • Production by Laura Grandi • Published by Rachel Williams

ISBN: 978-1-84780-865-3

Printed in China

1 3 5 7 9 8 6 4 2